Accelerated Christian Training Series

Laying the FOUNDATION

BOOK 7

THE EXALTATION OF CHRIST

Dr. Mark Hanby

© Copyright 2001 — Mark Hanby Ministries

All rights reserved. This book is protected by the copyright laws of the United States of America. This book may not be copied or reprinted for commercial gain or profit. The use of short quotations or occasional page copying for personal or group study is permitted and encouraged. Permission will be granted upon request. Unless otherwise identified, Scripture quotations are from the New King James Version of the Bible. Emphasis within Scripture quotations is the author's own. Please note that Destiny Image's publishing style capitalizes certain pronouns in Scripture that refer to the Father, Son, and Holy Spirit, and may differ from some Bible publishers' styles.

Take note that the name satan and related names are not capitalized. We choose not to acknowledge him, even to the point of violating grammatical rules.

Destiny Image® Publishers, Inc.
P.O. Box 310
Shippensburg, PA 17257-0310

"Speaking to the Purposes of God for This
Generation and for the Generations to Come"

ISBN 0-7684-2148-9

For Worldwide Distribution
Printed in the U.S.A.

This book and all other Destiny Image, Revival Press,
MercyPlace, Fresh Bread, Destiny Image Fiction,
and Treasure House books are available
at Christian bookstores and distributors worldwide.

For a U.S. bookstore nearest you, call **1-800-722-6774**.
For more information on foreign distributors,
call **717-532-3040**.
Or reach us on the Internet: **www.destinyimage.com**

Contents

	Introduction	**5**
I.	**The Exaltation of Christ**	**11**
	A. What Do the Scriptures Teach Us About Christ's Descent Into Hell?	
	B. What Is the Significance of the Resurrection of Christ?	
	C. What Assurances Do We Have As a Result of Christ's Resurrection?	
	D. What Is the Significance of Christ's Ascension?	
	E. How and When Will Christ Return to the Earth?	
	F. What Are We to Do Until Christ's Return?	
II.	**Jesus Christ and the Kingdom of God**	**24**
	A. What Is the Kingdom of God?	
	B. How Was the Kingdom Announced?	
	C. How Did Jesus Introduce the Kingdom of God?	
	D. How Was the Kingdom of God Manifested in the New Testament?	
	E. How was the Kingdom of God Described?	
	F. How Do We Enter the Kingdom of God?	
	Laying the Foundation Summary	**38**

Introduction

And you shall know the truth, and the truth shall make you free (John 8:32).

What Is Truth?

Truth Is a Person

"What is truth?" Pilate asked Jesus (Jn. 18:38). The answer to Pilate's timeless question was standing before him. Truth is not a series of facts or the sum of information. Truth is a Person: Jesus Christ. Jesus said of Himself, "I am the way, the truth, and the life" (Jn. 14:6). Truth is not only rational, it is relational. Religious theory that only teaches about God can never liberate the soul. True freedom is found in knowing Him. "And ye shall know the truth, and the truth shall make you free" (Jn. 8:32).

God has chosen to unfold His relational truth in various ways throughout the Bible and always in the form of personal relationship between Himself and men such as Adam, Noah, and Abraham. The unfolding revelation of God's relationship with man was spelled out in agreements between God and man called covenants. What better way to unfold a relational truth than in the context of relationship?

Truth Is the Result of Seeking Jesus

This relational truth is more than experience. Despite his great experience on the road to Damascus, the apostle Paul did not end his search for truth but wrote, "...that I may know *Him* and the power of His resurrection, and the fellowship of His sufferings..." (Phil. 3:10, emphasis mine). Job, wounded and in distress, cried out, "Oh that I knew where I might find *Him*..."

(Job 23:3). Jesus said, "Blessed are those who hunger and thirst for righteousness, for they shall be filled" (Mt. 5:6). Our finding the truth is the result of a hunger to know the Person of Jesus Christ. We do not seek truth and find Jesus; we seek Jesus and find the truth.

Truth Is a Highway

We may think of truth as a highway—an endless journey into the Person of God. All of us walking in the light of relationship with God are at some point in that journey. As we "seek the Lord" and "search the Scriptures," we advance. The **A**ccelerated **C**hristian **T**raining **S**eries has been created to help us move on in that journey into the Lord regardless of whether we are new believers or seasoned saints of God. There is always more truth for us regardless of our place along the road. "His ways [are] past finding out" (Rom. 11:33b).

It is important that every believer follow a course such as this. Although the believer may be exposed to a variety of good biblical preaching, there must be a systematic seeking after truth to provide a foundation upon which to grow in relationship with the Person of Jesus. Imagine agreeing to marry someone of whom you had only seen a pencil sketching. It is our intention in this course of seeking to paint a full and vital portrait of the Christ who is alive in you.

If you are a new traveler on the highway of truth, you have begun the most exciting journey of your life. Many parallels can be drawn between the new believer and a newborn child. It would be a criminal act to leave an infant out in the cold or in a house without someone to give him attention and care. It is likewise a tragedy when the Church does not nurture newborn Christians. If newborns are going to be healthy and grow to

Introduction

maturity, they must be carefully and loving fed with the truth of the word.

Truth Brings Maturity

The Christian life is a "growing up into Him in all things...until we come to the measure of the stature of the fullness of Christ" (see Eph. 4:13-15). It is important that we place ourselves under pastoral care if we are to "grow up." Even Jesus, who astonished the doctors and lawyers of His time, was entrusted to His parents' care. The Bible says, "Obey those who rule over you, and be submissive: for they watch out for your souls" (Heb. 13:17). To reject the care of pastoral oversight is to reject God's plan to bring us to Himself and to leave ourselves open to error and the exit from the highway of our journey into the truth.

The ministry that God has given to the Church is five-phased with a threefold purpose. Ephesians 4:11 tells us that God has placed in the church apostles, prophets, evangelists, pastors and teachers. Their purpose is to mature, feed and motivate believers in their own calling and ministry. Only when this equipping is established in the life of the believer will they progress from spiritual newborn to spiritual childhood and on to spiritual adulthood.

In the life of every Christian there must come a point where we "put away childish things" (1 Cor. 13:11). As we become "rooted and grounded" in the basic principles of faith we are "no more children, tossed to and fro, and carried about with every wind of doctrine" (Eph. 4:14). As we grow and mature in the faith we are able to rise above our own problems and trials and reach out with power and confidence to minister the truth to the needs of those around us.

The Exaltation of Christ

How the Accelerated Christian Training Series Works

The **A**ccelerated **C**hristian **T**raining **S**eries has been designed to meet the crucial need for intensive training in the basic doctrines of the Christian faith. These doctrines are revealed in the context of relationship between God and man. It is designed as a self-instruction course in which believers can journey at their own pace. You will find review questions at the end of each section of material you have studied that will help you to retain what you've learned.

There is an exercise called "Dig a Little Deeper; Grow a Little Closer" at the end of each major section. These reflective questions are designed to help you synthesize the truths you have been taught and then apply them in a personal way. You will be invited to journal throughout the study of this book to provide you with a record of your new understanding and growth in God. Journaling will help you to grow in your ability to hear God's voice and adjust your life and understanding to His purpose.

Following this **A.C.T.S.** course will stimulate and accelerate your spiritual understanding and bring you to a more intimate knowledge of the Truth, who is Jesus Christ. We pray that you will grow in the awareness of the Lord's presence as He guides you to Himself through the study of His Word.

Two Companions for the Road

During this time of new growth in your spiritual life there will be questions that come to mind. You will meet two companions throughout this series on the road to truth. They are Newly Newborn and Truly Taughtright. Newly will ask some of the same questions that you ask, and Truly, his mentor, will give the answers.

Introduction

From Cross to Crown to Kingdom

Behold, My Servant shall deal prudently; He shall be exalted and extolled and be very high (Isaiah 52:13).

Here we are, at the final chapter of God's plan to restore relationship between Himself and mankind. Jesus Christ, Son of God, Servant of God, has fulfilled all the requirements to bring us back to God. In the last section we learned that Jesus was the perfect and obedient servant of God's purpose. You and I now enter into His perfect faith and obedience to the Father. Now that He has accomplished the Father's mission He will establish His kingdom, made up of all those who recognize His great work of redemption. Through the life, death, resurrection, and ascension of Jesus Christ, we now have the power to be what God created us to be.

When we speak about the exaltation of Christ, we are speaking of all that took place after His crucifixion:

- His descending into hell
- His resurrection on the third day
- His ascension into heaven and sitting at the right hand of God
- His ultimate return to judge the alive and the dead

As you complete this final chapter, keep the following Scripture text in mind.

Let this mind be in you which was also in Christ Jesus, who, being in the form of God, did not consider it robbery to be equal with God, but made Himself of no reputation, taking the form of a bondservant, and coming

The Exaltation of Christ

in the likeness of men. And being found in appearance as a man, He humbled Himself and became obedient to the point of death, even the death of the cross. Therefore God also has highly exalted Him and given Him the name which is above every name, that at the name of Jesus every knee should bow, of those in heaven, and of those on earth, and of those under the earth, and that every tongue should confess that Jesus Christ is Lord, to the glory of God the Father (Philippians 2:5-11).

I. The Exaltation of Christ

A. **What Do the Scriptures Teach Us About Christ's Descent Into Hell?**

　　1.　Jesus, after His crucifixion, went to preach to spirits of people who died and were in Hades. They had an opportunity to accept Christ and be in the presence of God.

For Christ also suffered once for sins, the just for the unjust, that He might bring us to God, being put to death in the flesh but made alive by the Spirit, by whom also He went and preached to the spirits in prison (1 Peter 3:18-19).

For this reason the gospel was preached also to those who are dead, that they might be judged according to men in the flesh, but live according to God in the spirit (1 Peter 4:6).

　　2.　Jesus preached to those in Hades so that the gospel would be preached to all regions, and so that He might fill all things.

Therefore He says: "When He ascended on high, He led captivity captive, and gave gifts to men." (Now this, "He ascended"— what does it mean but that He also first descended into the lower parts of the earth? He who descended is also the One who ascended far above all the heavens, that He might fill all things.) (Ephesians 4:8-10).

B. **What Is the Significance of the Resurrection of Christ?**

　　1.　The Scriptures teach us that three days after Jesus died He was raised from the dead.

The Exaltation of Christ

And He began to teach them that the Son of Man must suffer many things, and be rejected by the elders and chief priests and scribes, and be killed, and after three days rise again (Mark 8:31).

And we are witnesses of all things which He did both in the land of the Jews and in Jerusalem, whom they killed by hanging on a tree. Him God raised up on the third day, and showed Him openly (Acts 10:39-40).

2. The Scriptures tell us that Christ was raised with a glorified physical body as the firstfruits from the dead. He had a body free of the corruption that resulted from the Fall of Adam.

But now Christ is risen from the dead, and has become the firstfruits of those who have fallen asleep. For since by man came death, by Man also came the resurrection of the dead. For as in Adam all die, even so in Christ all shall be made alive (1 Corinthians 15:20-22).

So also is the resurrection of the dead. The body is sown in corruption, it is raised in incorruption. It is sown in dishonor, it is raised in glory. It is sown in weakness, it is raised in power. It is sown a natural body, it is raised a spiritual body. There is a natural body, and there is a spiritual body (1 Corinthians 15:42-44).

C. What Assurances Do We Have As a Result of Christ's Resurrection?

1. The resurrection assures us that Jesus Christ is the Son of God.

The Exaltation of Christ

God has fulfilled this for us their children, in that He has raised up Jesus. As it is also written in the second Psalm: "You are My Son, today I have begotten You" (Acts 13:33).

And declared to be the Son of God with power according to the Spirit of holiness, by the resurrection from the dead (Romans 1:4).

2. The resurrection assures us that all of the words Jesus spoke were true.

Jesus answered and said to them, "Destroy this temple, and in three days I will raise it up." Then the Jews said, "It has taken forty-six years to build this temple, and will you raise it up in three days?" But He was speaking of the temple of His body (John 2:19-21).

3. The resurrection assures us that the Father approved His work of redemption and accepted His sacrifice.

But also for us. It shall be imputed to us who believe in Him who raised up Jesus our Lord from the dead, who was delivered up because of our offenses, and was raised because of our justification (Romans 4:24-25).

4. The resurrection assures us that believers in Christ have the hope of eternal life.

Blessed be the God and Father of our Lord Jesus Christ, who according to His abundant mercy has begotten us again to a living hope through the

The Exaltation of Christ

resurrection of Jesus Christ from the dead (1 Peter 1:3).

5. It assures us that believers will receive perfect and incorruptible bodies like Jesus.

So also is the resurrection of the dead. The body is sown in corruption, it is raised in incorruption. It is sown in dishonor, it is raised in glory. It is sown in weakness, it is raised in power. It is sown a natural body, it is raised a spiritual body. There is a natural body, and there is a spiritual body (1 Corinthians 15:42-44).

For our citizenship is in heaven, from which we also eagerly wait for the Savior, the Lord Jesus Christ, who will transform our lowly body that it may be conformed to His glorious body, according to the working by which He is able even to subdue all things to Himself (Philippians 3:20-21).

D. What Is the Significance of Christ's Ascension?

1. The ascension of Christ is significant in that He leads the way for us into the glory of God.

Father, I desire that they also whom You gave Me may be with Me where I am, that they may behold My glory which You have given Me; for You loved Me before the foundation of the world (John 17:24).

For it was fitting for Him, for whom are all things and by whom are all things, in bringing many

The Exaltation of Christ

sons to glory, to make the captain of their salvation perfect through sufferings (Hebrews 2:10).

Where the forerunner has entered for us, even Jesus, having become High Priest forever according to the order of Melchizedek (Hebrews 6:20).

2. The ascension of Christ is significant in that He received honor and glory, being seated at the right hand of God. This is the place of all authority and power.

Jesus said to him, "It is as you said. Nevertheless, I say to you, hereafter you will see the Son of Man sitting at the right hand of the Power..." (Matthew 26:64).

And Jesus came and spoke to them, saying, "All authority has been given to Me in heaven and on earth" (Matthew 28:18).

And you are complete in Him, who is the head of all principality and power (Colossians 2:10).

3. The ascension of Christ to the right hand of God means that all other powers have been put under His feet.

The Lord said to my Lord, "Sit at My right hand, till I make Your enemies Your footstool" (Psalm 110:1).

Which He worked in Christ when He raised Him from the dead and seated Him at His right hand in the heavenly places, far above all principality and power and might and dominion, and every name that is named, not only in this age but also in that

The Exaltation of Christ

which is to come. And He put all things under His feet, and gave Him to be head over all things to the church, which is His body, the fullness of Him who fills all in all (Ephesians 1:20-23).

Therefore God also has highly exalted Him and given Him the name which is above every name, that at the name of Jesus every knee should bow, of those in heaven, and of those on earth, and of those under the earth, and that every tongue should confess that Jesus Christ is Lord, to the glory of God the Father (Philippians 2:9-11).

Who has gone into heaven and is at the right hand of God, angels and authorities and powers having been made subject to Him (1 Peter 3:22).

4. The ascension of Christ gives us hope of living eternally in a place prepared for us by the Lord Himself.

Simon Peter said to Him, "Lord, where are You going?" Jesus answered him, "Where I am going you cannot follow Me now, but you shall follow Me afterward" (John 13:36).

Father, I desire that they also whom You gave Me may be with Me where I am, that they may behold My glory which You have given Me; for You loved Me before the foundation of the world (John 17:24).

5. The ascension of Christ assures us that we will rule and reign with Him.

Even when we were dead in trespasses, made us alive together with Christ (by grace you have been saved), and raised us up together, and made us sit together in the heavenly places in Christ Jesus, that in the ages to come He might show the exceeding riches of His grace in His kindness toward us in Christ Jesus (Ephesians 2:5-7).

6. The ascension of Christ provides a new focus on the throne of God rather than the circumstances of our earthly life.

If then you were raised with Christ, seek those things which are above, where Christ is, sitting at the right hand of God. Set your mind on things above, not on things on the earth (Colossians 3:1-2).

For to be carnally minded is death, but to be spiritually minded is life and peace (Romans 8:6).

While we do not look at the things which are seen, but at the things which are not seen. For the things which are seen are temporary, but the things which are not seen are eternal (2 Corinthians 4:18).

For our citizenship is in heaven, from which we also eagerly wait for the Savior, the Lord Jesus Christ, who will transform our lowly body that it may be conformed to His glorious body, according to the working by which He is able even to subdue all things to Himself (Philippians 3:20-21).

E. **How and When Will Christ Return to the Earth?**

1. Christ will return to the earth in the same glory with which He ascended.

The Exaltation of Christ

For the Son of Man will come in the glory of His Father with His angels, and then He will reward each according to his works (Matthew 16:27).

And while they looked steadfastly toward heaven as He went up, behold, two men stood by them in white apparel, who also said, "Men of Galilee, why do you stand gazing up into heaven? This same Jesus, who was taken up from you into heaven, will so come in like manner as you saw Him go into heaven" (Acts 1:10-11).

2. Christ will return in righteous judgment of the living and the dead.

Truly, these times of ignorance God overlooked, but now commands all men everywhere to repent, because He has appointed a day on which He will judge the world in righteousness by the Man whom He has ordained. He has given assurance of this to all by raising Him from the dead (Acts 17:30-31).

3. Christ will return at a time known only by God. We are to watch for His return.

Watch therefore, for you know neither the day nor the hour in which the Son of Man is coming (Matthew 25:13).

But the day of the Lord will come as a thief in the night, in which the heavens will pass away with a great noise, and the elements will melt with fervent heat; both the earth and the works that are in it will be burned up (2 Peter 3:10).

The Exaltation of Christ

F. What Are We to Do Until Christ's Return?

We are to do the business of the kingdom until Christ's return.

So he called ten of his servants, delivered to them ten minas, and said to them, "Do business till I come" (Luke 19:13).

Let's Review What We Have Learned About the Exaltation of Jesus Christ.

1. What four things are we talking about when we discuss the exaltation of Jesus Christ?

_____

_____

_____

_____

2. The _____ assures us that Jesus Christ is the Son of God.

3. The resurrection assures us that believers in Christ have the hope of _____.

4. The right hand of God is the place of all _____ and _____.

5. The ascension of Christ provides a new focus on the _____ of God rather than the _____ of our earthly life.

6. Christ will return in righteous judgment of the _____ and the _____.

The Exaltation of Christ

Dig a Little Deeper; Grow a Little Closer

1. Read the verses below and respond to the questions that follow.

> *Which He worked in Christ when He raised Him from the dead and seated Him at His right hand in the heavenly places, far above all principality and power and might and dominion, and every name that is named, not only in this age but also in that which is to come. And He put all things under His feet, and gave Him to be head over all things to the church, which is His body, the fullness of Him who fills all in all...Even when we were dead in trespasses, made us alive together with Christ (by grace you have been saved), and raised us up together, and made us sit together in the heavenly places in Christ Jesus, that in the ages to come He might show the exceeding riches of His grace in His kindness toward us in Christ Jesus* (Ephesians 1:20-23; 5:2-7).

2. Where do these verses tell us that Christ is right now? What has been put under His feet?

_____

_____

_____

3. Look at Ephesians 2:6. Where does this verse tell us that believers are seated?

_____

_____

_____

The Exaltation of Christ

4. Given the reality of these verses toward believers, what new perspective do you gain that might help you when you experience difficulties in life?

_____

_____

_____

The Exaltation of Christ

Review Notes

The Exaltation of Christ

II. Jesus Christ and the Kingdom of God

A. **What Is the Kingdom of God?**

1. The Kingdom of God is the present reality of God's rule over all who submit to His Lordship.

Now when He was asked by the Pharisees when the kingdom of God would come, He answered them and said, "The kingdom of God does not come with observation; nor will they say, 'See here!' or 'See there!' For indeed, the kingdom of God is within you" (Luke 17:20-21).

Jesus answered and said to him, "Most assuredly, I say to you, unless one is born again, he cannot see the kingdom of God" (John 3:3).

Listen, my beloved brethren: Has God not chosen the poor of this world to be rich in faith and heirs of the kingdom which He promised to those who love Him? (James 2:5)

2. The Kingdom of God is the realm of His sovereign authority and dominion. This realm will continue to increase until all is subjected to Jesus Christ as King.

Your kingdom is an everlasting kingdom, and Your dominion endures throughout all generations (Psalm 145:13).

Then the seventh angel sounded: And there were loud voices in heaven, saying, "The kingdoms of this world have become the kingdoms of our Lord

Jesus Christ and the Kingdom of God

and of His Christ, and He shall reign forever and ever!" (Revelation 11:15)

3. The Kingdom of God is ruled by Jesus Christ the King.

Now Jesus stood before the governor. And the governor asked Him, saying, "Are You the King of the Jews?" So Jesus said to him, "It is as you say" (Matthew 27:11).

Now to the King eternal, immortal, invisible, to God who alone is wise, be honor and glory forever and ever. Amen (1 Timothy 1:17).

B.   How Was the Kingdom Announced?

1. The Kingdom of God was announced in the Old Testament.

The Lord is good to all, and His tender mercies are over all His works. All Your works shall praise You, O Lord, and Your saints shall bless You. They shall speak of the glory of Your kingdom, and talk of Your power, to make known to the sons of men His mighty acts, and the glorious majesty of His kingdom. Your kingdom is an everlasting kingdom, and Your dominion endures throughout all generations (Psalm 145:9-13).

I was watching in the night visions, and behold, One like the Son of Man, coming with the clouds of heaven! He came to the Ancient of Days, and they brought Him near before Him. Then to Him was given dominion and glory and a kingdom, that all peoples, nations, and languages should

The Exaltation of Christ

serve Him. His dominion is an everlasting dominion, which shall not pass away, and His kingdom the one which shall not be destroyed...But the saints of the Most High shall receive the kingdom, and possess the kingdom forever, even forever and ever...Then the kingdom and dominion, and the greatness of the kingdoms under the whole heaven, shall be given to the people, the saints of the Most High. His kingdom is an everlasting kingdom, and all dominions shall serve and obey Him (Daniel 7:13-14,18,27).

The law and the prophets were until John. Since that time the kingdom of God has been preached, and everyone is pressing into it (Luke 16:16).

2. The Kingdom of God was announced in the New Testament.

In those days John the Baptist came preaching in the wilderness of Judea, and saying, "Repent, for the kingdom of heaven is at hand!" (Matthew 3:1-2)

Now after John was put in prison, Jesus came to Galilee, preaching the gospel of the kingdom of God, and saying, "The time is fulfilled, and the kingdom of God is at hand. Repent, and believe in the gospel" (Mark 1:14-15).

Then the angel said to her, "Do not be afraid, Mary, for you have found favor with God. And behold, you will conceive in your womb and bring forth a Son, and shall call His name Jesus. He will be great, and will be called the Son of the Highest; and the Lord God will give Him the throne of His father David. And He will reign over the house of

Jesus Christ and the Kingdom of God

Jacob forever, and of His kingdom there will be no end" (Luke 1:30-33).

C. **How Did Jesus Introduce the Kingdom of God?**

  1. Jesus preached the Kingdom of God from the very beginning of His ministry.

But He said to them, "I must preach the kingdom of God to the other cities also, because for this purpose I have been sent." And He was preaching in the synagogues of Galilee (Luke 4:43-44).

Now after John was put in prison, Jesus came to Galilee, preaching the gospel of the kingdom of God, and saying, "The time is fulfilled, and the kingdom of God is at hand. Repent, and believe in the gospel" (Mark 1:14-15).

  2. Jesus preached that the Kingdom of God had come as a present reality, not just a hope for the future. The prophecies concerning the Kingdom were now fulfilled in Christ.

From that time Jesus began to preach and to say, "Repent, for the kingdom of heaven is at hand."...And Jesus went about all Galilee, teaching in their synagogues, preaching the gospel of the kingdom, and healing all kinds of sickness and all kinds of disease among the people (Matthew 4:17,23).

"The Spirit of the Lord is upon Me, because He has anointed Me to preach the gospel to the poor; He

has sent Me to heal the brokenhearted, to proclaim liberty to the captives and recovery of sight to the blind, to set at liberty those who are oppressed; to proclaim the acceptable year of the Lord." Then He closed the book, and gave it back to the attendant and sat down. And the eyes of all who were in the synagogue were fixed on Him. And He began to say to them, "Today this Scripture is fulfilled in your hearing" (Luke 4:18-21).

D. How Was the Kingdom of God Manifested in the New Testament?

1. The Kingdom of God was manifested in the ministry of Jesus Christ.

Then Jesus went about all the cities and villages, teaching in their synagogues, preaching the gospel of the kingdom, and healing every sickness and every disease among the people (Matthew 9:35).

2. The Kingdom of God was manifested by authority over sickness and demons.

And as you go, preach, saying, "The kingdom of heaven is at hand." Heal the sick, cleanse the lepers, raise the dead, cast out demons. Freely you have received, freely give (Matthew 10:7-8).

But if I cast out demons by the Spirit of God, surely the kingdom of God has come upon you (Matthew 12:28).

Then He called His twelve disciples together and gave them power and authority over all demons, and to cure diseases. He sent them to preach the kingdom of God and to heal the sick (Luke 9:1-2).

3.   The Kingdom of God was manifested in the outpouring of the Holy Spirit. The Church became witness of the reality of Christ's enthronement and present rule.

But to each one of us grace was given according to the measure of Christ's gift. Therefore He says: "When He ascended on high, He led captivity captive, and gave gifts to men" (Ephesians 4:7-8).

When the Day of Pentecost had fully come, they were all with one accord in one place. And suddenly there came a sound from heaven, as of a rushing mighty wind, and it filled the whole house where they were sitting. Then there appeared to them divided tongues, as of fire, and one sat upon each of them. And they were all filled with the Holy Spirit and began to speak with other tongues, as the Spirit gave them utterance... "Therefore, being a prophet, and knowing that God had sworn with an oath to him that of the fruit of his body, according to the flesh, He would raise up the Christ to sit on his throne, he, foreseeing this, spoke concerning the resurrection of the Christ, that His soul was not left in Hades, nor did His flesh see corruption. This Jesus God has raised up, of which we are all witnesses. Therefore being exalted to the right hand of God, and having received from the Father the promise of the Holy Spirit, He poured out this which you now see and hear. For David did not ascend into the heavens, but he says himself: 'The Lord said to my Lord,

The Exaltation of Christ

"Sit at My right hand, till I make Your enemies Your footstool"'" (Acts 2:1-4,30-35).

E. How Was the Kingdom of God Described?

   1. The Kingdom of God is described in the Sermon on the Mount and the Beatitudes found in Matthew 5. (What we are "to be" in the Kingdom).

Blessed are the poor in spirit, for theirs is the kingdom of heaven. Blessed are those who mourn, for they shall be comforted. Blessed are the meek, for they shall inherit the earth. Blessed are those who hunger and thirst for righteousness, for they shall be filled. Blessed are the merciful, for they shall obtain mercy. Blessed are the pure in heart, for they shall see God. Blessed are the peacemakers, for they shall be called sons of God. Blessed are those who are persecuted for righteousness' sake, for theirs is the kingdom of heaven. Blessed are you when they revile and persecute you, and say all kinds of evil against you falsely for My sake (Matthew 5:3-11).

   2. The Kingdom of God is described in the parables Jesus taught.

Then He said, "To what shall we liken the kingdom of God? Or with what parable shall we picture it? It is like a mustard seed which, when it is sown on the ground, is smaller than all the seeds on earth; but when it is sown, it grows up and becomes greater than all herbs, and shoots out large branches, so that the birds of the air may nest under its shade. And with many such

Jesus Christ and the Kingdom of God

parables He spoke the word to them as they were able to hear it (Mark 4:30-33).

F. How Do We Enter the Kingdom of God?

1. We enter the Kingdom of God by trusting Jesus Christ as Lord and Savior. Those called into the Kingdom are the *ekklesia*, the Church. The Church is the community of those who respond to God's calling into the Kingdom.

Praising God and having favor with all the people. And the Lord added to the church daily those who were being saved (Acts 2:47).

2. We enter the Kingdom by obedience to the King, Jesus Christ.

Not everyone who says to Me, "Lord, Lord," shall enter the kingdom of heaven, but he who does the will of My Father in heaven (Matthew 7:21).

The Exaltation of Christ

And from the days of John the Baptist until now the kingdom of heaven suffers violence, and the violent take it by force (Matthew 11:12).

Let's Review What We Have Learned About the Kingdom of God.

1. The Kingdom of God is the present reality of God's _____ over all who submit to His _____.

2. Jesus preached that the Kingdom of God had come as a _____, not just a hope for the _____. The prophecies concerning the Kingdom were now _____ in Christ.

3. List two ways that the Kingdom of God was manifested in the New Testament.

_____

_____

4. We enter the Kingdom of God by _____ Jesus Christ as _____ and _____.

5. What position does Jesus Christ hold in the Kingdom of God?

_____

_____

_____

6. The Church became the _____ of the reality of Christ's _____ and present rule.

Jesus Christ and the Kingdom of God

Dig a Little Deeper; Grow a Little Closer

1. Read the verses below and respond to the questions that follow.

Again, the kingdom of heaven is like a merchant seeking beautiful pearls, who, when he had found one pearl of great price, went and sold all that he had and bought it (Matthew 13:45-46).

2. What were some things that were valuable to you before you came to Christ or began this book? List them here.

_____

_____

_____

_____

3. Take the list above and compare those items with your salvation and relationship with Jesus Christ. How has your new understanding changed how you value these things?

_____

_____

_____

_____

_____

Don't forget to journal what the Lord has spoken to you in this chapter. Now that you are at the end of the book, look back and see how the Lord has been speaking to you and where He has led you. Give Him praise for the new reality of your salvation. May the Lord richly bless you as you continue to grow in Him.

The Exaltation of Christ

—A Final Word on the Church of Jesus Christ—

The Church of Jesus Christ is the community of those who have entered into His reign. The Church is not the Kingdom but all those in the true Church are in the Kingdom. In the Church all the major themes of God's redemptive efforts are seen. The Church is the ultimate example of the "remnant" that we spoke of much earlier. They are the ones to whom all the promises of God are conveyed. If you have not yet entered the Kingdom of God through faith in Jesus Christ, now is the time. Pray this prayer:

> *Lord, I know that I am a sinner, hopelessly lost and unable to live for You in my own strength. I desire to enter into Your Kingdom by means of the sacrifice You made for me. I believe that You can do all that I cannot do. I acknowledge Jesus Christ as my own Lord, Savior and King. I ask You to fill me now with your Holy Spirit and enable me to live in an intimate relationship with You through faith in and obedience to Jesus Christ, my Lord and my God. Amen!*

Jesus Christ and the Kingdom of God

Review Notes

The Exaltation of Christ

Jesus Christ and the Kingdom of God

Be sure to enter into the journal in this book how God responds to what you have prayed.

Laying the Foundation Summary
Book 1—The Nature of God

I. **The Nature of God**

    A. **Who Is God?**

        God is the Creator and sustainer of all things.

    B. **How Is It Possible for Man to Know God?**

        1. We can know God because He dwells in His own creation.

        2. God's desire is to fellowship with all men as He did at first with Adam.

        3. God can be seen in what He has created. God spoke all the laws of nature into existence at the very beginning.

        4. God has given us His Holy Scriptures, the Bible, to come to know Him.

    C. **What Is God?**

        God is a Spirit; He is without flesh and blood and is invisible to us.

    D. **What Qualities Might We Use to Describe God?**

        1. God is omnipotent; He is all-powerful, able to do anything.

        2. God is omniscient; He is all-knowing. He knows all about me, what I think and where I am going.

        3. God is omnipresent; He is present in all places and times at once.

        4. God is eternal; He lives outside of time and space.

        5. God never changes.

        6. God is holy; He is utterly pure, without sin, without darkness.

Laying the Foundation Summary

    7.   God is just and fair to all people.

    8.   God is faithful; He will always do what He says He will do.

    9.   God is good; He wants only the very best for us.

    10.   God is full of mercy; He delivers us from the bondage of sin and death.

    11.   God is gracious; He shows us undeserved kindness; He does for us what we cannot do for ourselves.

    12.   God is infinite; He is beyond measure and bigger than anything we can see.

    13.   God is love.

E.   **What Does the Term *Triune Godhead* Mean?**

    1.   God has revealed Himself in three manifestations (some people use the term *persons*)—Father, Son, and Holy Spirit. He is Father in creation, Son in redemption, and Holy Spirit in regeneration.

    2.   When we reach Heaven we will see only one God manifested as Father, Son, and Holy Spirit. A man can be father, son, and a husband all at the same time but still only one man.

F.   **What Is God's Name?**

    1.   There are many names for God throughout the Bible that tell us something about God, but God's name for Himself is *Yahweh* or *Yah*. This word could be translated "I AM." The English version of *Yahweh* is Jehovah. In His name God has revealed Himself as the "Great I AM."

    2.   God's name for Himself was holy and never pronounced by the people of Israel. Instead they substituted the word *LORD*. Wherever we see the word *LORD* in all capital letters in our Bibles, the original Hebrew word was the name *Yahweh*.

    3.   Jesus also refers to Himself as "I AM," the same as the Father.

The Exaltation of Christ

G. **What Is the Difference Between the Lord of the Old Testament and the Lord of the New Testament?**

    1. They are the same. The Lord of the Old Testament came in the flesh in the New Testament in the Person of the Lord Jesus Christ.

    2. The Lord speaks of Himself using the same terms in both the Old and the New Testaments.

    3. *Jesus* is the New Testament name for God. The name *Jesus* means, "Jehovah has become salvation." Jesus commissioned the disciples to baptize in the name of the Father, the Son, and the Holy Spirit. The apostles obeyed this commission by baptizing in the name of Jesus Christ.

H. **Who Is the Holy Spirit and How Is He Related to Jesus Christ?**

    1. Jesus is identified with the Holy Spirit because of the Spirit's activity in His life and ministry. The Holy Spirit is the anointing of God. The Greek word for anointing is the same word from which we get the word *Christ*.

    2. The same Holy Spirit who was active in the life and ministry of Jesus Christ was released into His Body on earth, the Church, when He ascended to Heaven.

    3. The Holy Spirit and the Spirit of Christ are the same Person, dwelling in His Body, the Church.

II. **The Bible**

  A. **What Is the Bible?**

    1. The Bible is the inspired or "God-breathed" word of God.

    2. The Holy Spirit moved upon the holy men who wrote the Bible.

Laying the Foundation Summary

3. Every word of the Bible is God's; therefore the Bible is without error.

4. The Bible is given to us to give us wisdom that leads to salvation through faith in Christ Jesus.

5. The Bible enables us to live a holy life.

6. The Bible tells us about Jesus Christ.

7. The Bible is the testimony of God that, when read, renews our minds. As we search the Scriptures diligently and reverently and listen while they are being read, they guide us in our daily living.

B. **What Are the Results of Obeying the Bible?**

1. As we obey the Bible we are blessed.

2. As we obey the Bible we display our love for Jesus.

3. As we obey the Bible we avoid sin.

C. **What Are the Two Great Divisions in the Bible?**

1. The first part of the Bible is the Old Testament, which contains the Law. The Law is a guideline that teaches us how to live in harmony with God and man. It is the basis for all government.

2. The second part of the Bible is called the New Testament. It contains the Gospel, which is the good news of our salvation in Christ Jesus.

3. The difference between the Law and the Gospel is that the Law teaches what man can and cannot do, and the Gospel teaches what God has done and still does. The Law shows us our sin, but the Gospel shows us God's grace through Jesus Christ.

D. **What Are the Books of the Bible?**

1. The Bible is not a single book but a collection of 66 books written under the inspiration of the Holy

The Exaltation of Christ

Spirit by 44 different writers. The books of the Bible were written over a period of 2,000 years, yet its books provide a perfect harmony of doctrines.

2. There are many different kinds of books in the Bible.

E. What Are the Benefits of Studying the Bible?

1. Studying the Bible uncovers sin.

2. Studying the Bible cleanses us from the pollution of sin.

3. Studying the Bible gives us strength for our lives.

4. Studying the Bible gives us direction for our lives.

5. Studying the Bible provides us a sword for victory over sin.

6. Studying the Bible gives us power to pray.

F. How Often Should We Read From This Collection of Books?

We should read from the Bible every day.

G. What Other Books Should Supplement My Study of the Bible?

1. A good Bible dictionary, which defines various words and subjects of the Bible

2. An exhaustive concordance, which shows us where certain words occur throughout the Bible

3. A Bible handbook, which gives a general background and commentary on the passages we are reading

H. What Should We Do After Reading the Bible?

We should meditate on what we have read, then soak in its truths and allow them to become part of us.

Laying the Foundation Summary

III. **The Creation**

    A. **What Did God Create?**

        God created all that is seen and unseen; everything that is in Heaven and earth; the spirit realm and the natural realm.

    B. **What Did God Create First?**

        God created the heavens, the unseen realm of angels or ministering spirits.

    C. **What Are Angels?**

        1. Angels are invisible ministering spirits created by God to do His will.

        2. There are good angels and evil angels.

    D. **What Does the Bible Tell Us About Good Angels?**

        1. Good angels are greater in number and power than evil angels.

        2. Good angels praise God.

        3. Good angels carry out God's commands and serve God's purpose, especially among children.

    E. **What Does the Bible Tell Us About Evil Angels?**

        1. Evil angels were created to be holy but rebelled against God and are now separated from Him forever.

        2. Evil angels are cunning, powerful, and great in number.

        3. Evil angels are the enemies of God and also of man. They endeavor to destroy the works of God.

    F. **Are Angels to Be Worshiped?**

        1. No. We are forbidden to worship angels.

The Exaltation of Christ

        2.   It is dangerous to become angel conscious. Even an angel can lead us astray.

G. Who Is Lucifer?

        1.   Lucifer was the chief angel of heaven. He was also called the "son of the morning." He was an anointed cherub of God covering the throne of God. But he rebelled against God and was cast out of heaven.

        2.   Lucifer was created beautiful. His appearance was as precious stones and his voice sounded like a great pipe organ. He was perfect in beauty and wisdom.

        3.   Lucifer became the devil, satan, and those that followed him became demons.

        4.   Lucifer and his demons are forever fallen from heaven. Some are held in everlasting chains and others roam the earth as enemies of God and man.

H. What Is Hell?

Hell is the abode of the devil and his demons. Only those who refuse Christ go to hell because there is no other place for them to go.

I. Who Has Power Over Satan and His Demons?

God and the Church of Jesus Christ have power and authority over satan and all his demons.

J. What Did God Create After the Spirit Realm?

        1.   In six days God created the physical universe that we can see.

        2.   God formed all living creatures on the earth.

        3.   God created man in His own image and gave him dominion over all of the earth. Man was unique in that God breathed His own breath of life into him and made him spiritually alive.

Laying the Foundation Summary

4. God created man as a special creation, not as the product of evolution. God made man alive with His very breath so that man would seek after God.

Book 2—The Nature of Man

I. **The Nature of Man**

   A. **Who Were Adam and Eve?**

      1. Adam and Eve were the first man and woman created by God and placed on the earth.

      2. Just as God Himself is one God with three parts, God created Adam as a three-part being: flesh by which he relates to the world, soul by which he relates to himself, and spirit by which he can relate to God.

   B. **For What Purpose Did God Create Adam and Eve?**

      1. Adam and Eve were created to glorify God and give Him pleasure.

      2. Adam and Eve were created to have an intimate relationship with God.

      3. Adam and Eve were created to have dominion over all other creatures.

      4. Adam and Eve were created to care for the garden in which God had placed them.

   C. **Why Did God Create Both a Man and a Woman?**

      1. God created both Adam and Eve because Adam could not fulfill God's purpose by himself. Eve was created as a "help meet."

      2. God created both Adam and Eve so that they could set an example for all future husbands and wives in their love for each other.

      3. God created Adam and Eve and gave them the power of creation to populate the earth.

The Exaltation of Christ

    D. What Agreement Did God Make With Man?

        1. God said He would provide man with all that he needed for life. Man was to depend totally upon God's power and wisdom for his life.

        2. Man was not to eat from the tree of the knowledge of good and evil and thus be independent from God. If he did he would be separated from God and would die spiritually.

II. The Fall of Man

    A. How Did Sin Enter the World?

        1. Sin entered into the world through Adam's choice to rebel against God's agreement and be independent from God.

        2. Sin entered the world when satan, in the form of a serpent, created doubt in Eve's mind about what God said.

        3. Sin entered the world as satan created doubt as to the provision of God.

        4. Sin entered into the world as satan created doubt as to man's relationship and dependence upon God.

        5. Sin still enters through these same areas of temptation: the lust of the flesh, the lust of the eyes, and the pride of life.

    B. What Was Man's True Sin at the Fall?

        1. Man's true sin was disobedience in acting on his own, independent of God, which is an act of rebellion.

        2. Man's true sin was taking his life into his own hands.

    C. What Was the Result of Man's Rebellion Against God?

        1. As a result of rebellion their eyes were opened and they knew they were naked.

Laying the Foundation Summary

        2. As a result of rebellion shame entered into the world.

        3. As a result of rebellion they sewed fig leaves to provide a covering for their shame.

        4. As a result of rebellion they tried to hide from the presence of God among the trees of the garden. Fear had entered into the world.

D. What Was the Result of Sin Entering Into the World?

The result of the entrance of sin into the world was separation from God and spiritual death. (See Romans 6:23.)

E. What of the Nature of God Is Revealed in His Response to Fallen Man?

        1. The justice of God is revealed in the pronunciation of three curses upon those in the garden.

        2. The mercy of God was revealed in that while God knew that Adam sinned He still came looking for him.

        3. The grace of God is revealed in His provision for covering the shame of Adam and Eve's sin.

F. Why Did God Send Man out of the Garden?

God sent man out of the garden so that he could not eat of the tree of life and live forever in his fallen condition, forever separated from God.

G. How Is It That All Men Are Born Under the Curse of Sin That Adam Committed?

All men are descended from Adam, who chose to rebel against God and forfeit the blessings of intimate relationship with God for which he was created.

III. The Seed of Rebellion Continues

    A. What Was Man's Attitude After He Sinned in the Garden?

        1. Man's attitude was one of rebellion. He wanted to be free from God.

The Exaltation of Christ

    2.   Man believed that he had a better way to meet his needs than God did.

    3.   Man believed the words of the serpent, that he could be like God.

B. **What Were the Effects of Rebellion After the Garden?**

    1.   Adam and Eve's first cooperative effort—the birth of Cain—produced the fruit of man's rebellion. The seed of rebellion that was planted in Adam led to murder in only one generation when Cain killed his brother Abel.

    2.   Rebellion and evil increased among men to the extent that God could no longer tolerate it.

    3.   God had no choice but to destroy the man whom He had created. He would destroy man by a great flood.

C. **How Would God's Purpose in Man Continue?**

    1.   Everyone on the earth was not to be destroyed. A man called Noah, righteous in his generation, found grace in the eyes of God.

    2.   In Noah, man would get a second chance. In Noah we learn the principle that God always preserves a remnant through which His purpose is performed.

D. **What Did God Command Noah to Do?**

    1.   God gave Noah instructions to build an ark—a large boat—to save himself, his family, and the animal life God had created.

    2.   Noah obeyed God in every detail.

E. **How Did Noah Acknowledge God's Authority Over His Life After He Came out of the Ark?**

    1.   Noah built an altar upon which to offer a sacrifice to the Lord.

    2.   As a result of Noah's acknowledgment of God's authority, God renewed His promise to man.

Laying the Foundation Summary

       3.   As a result of Noah's acknowledgment God renewed His purpose in man to fill the earth.

       4.   God gave the sign of the rainbow to confirm the promises He made to Noah.

F. What Was Man's Response to This New Beginning Following the Obedience of Noah?

       1.   Man responded with more rebellion. The sinful nature that resulted from the rebellion of Adam was still in man.

       2.   Man continued to rebel against authority as Ham, the son of Noah, shamelessly looked upon his father, who was uncovered, and made him an object of ridicule before the other sons.

G. How Did Man, With His Knowledge of Good and Evil, Begin to Build a New World?

       1.   Man continued his rebellion. Nimrod, a mighty hunter and a descendant of Noah's son Ham, began to build the Babylonian civilization.

       2.   Man began to build human civilization without God's wisdom and authority. He built a great city and a great tower to accomplish his own purpose.

       3.   Man built the great tower out of his desire to be independent from God. He wanted to build a great empire that would glorify man rather than God.

       4.   Man attempted to reach into heaven just as satan had tried to ascend to the throne of God in his own rebellion. Man deliberately opposed the charge of God to fill the earth by consolidating in one place.

H. Why and How Did God Stop the Building of the City and the Tower?

       1.   God stopped the building because of His wrath against man's rebellion. God hates the independent nature of man that thinks he can make it on his own.

The Exaltation of Christ

2. God stopped the building because man's rebellion could spread like an infection to all men. Man with the knowledge he had would continue to build and grow farther away from God.

3. God stopped man's rebellious building by confusing their language and scattering them throughout the earth. This ended the concentration of rebellion and evil.

4. God stopped the building of Babel, which means "the gate of god." Their city and its tower was their way to God. Babel in God's language means "confusion" or "mingle."

I. **What Is the Spiritual Meaning of Babylon to Us?**

1. The tower was built to glorify human wisdom and independence from God. The substitution of human government and wisdom in place of God's revelation through His Word will always fail.

2. We must seek to totally restore biblical Christianity—the one true faith.

3. We must be separated from man-made religion (Babylonian systems). We are to look to the Bible for direction and not human wisdom. We must allow the Holy Spirit to lead us into God's way and away from man's way.

Book 3—A Call to Faith and Obedience

I. **Abraham: The Father of Faith and Obedience**

   A. **Who Was Abraham?**

   1. Abraham was a man called into relationship with God.

   2. Abraham was a man who believed God.

   3. Abraham was a man who obeyed God.

Laying the Foundation Summary

       4.   Abraham was called a "friend of God" who walked in intimate fellowship with God.

       5.   Abraham was the father of all who inherit the promises of God by faith.

B.   What Did God Promise to Abraham?

       1.   God promised to make Abraham a great nation.

       2.   God promised to bless Abraham.

       3.   God promised to make Abraham's name great.

       4.   God promised to make Abraham a blessing.

       5.   God promised to bless those who blessed Abraham.

       6.   God promised to curse those who cursed Abraham.

       7.   God promised to bless all the families of the earth through Abraham.

       8.   God promised to give the land to Abraham's descendants.

       9.   God promised that Abraham's descendants would be numerous.

      10.   God promised that Abraham would be the father of many nations.

      11.   God promised that kings would be in Abraham's line.

      12.   God promised victory to Abraham against his enemies.

C.   What Did God Require of Abraham?

       1.   God required Abraham to leave his country.

       2.   God required Abraham to leave his family.

       3.   God required Abraham to leave his father's house.

       4.   God required Abraham to go to a land He would show him.

The Exaltation of Christ

D. **What Is a Covenant?**

1. A covenant is an agreement that binds two or more parties to each other in relationship. Each party agrees to fulfill certain conditions and each enjoys advantages as a result.

2. In covenant both parties agree on the terms and conditions for agreement. An example would be the marriage covenant or an employment contract.

E. **How Did God Make a Covenant With Abraham?**

1. God made a covenant with Abraham in which He set forth all the terms and bound Himself to fulfill the covenant.

2. God established the terms of the covenant with Abraham. God is superior to man and therefore God sets forth the terms. Man must choose either to accept or reject God's offer.

3. God guaranteed the covenant with the shedding of animal blood, which represented an exchanging of life.

4. God required the sign of circumcision of Abraham to demonstrate that he had accepted God's offer of covenant relationship. This included all Abraham's sons, male servants, and all other men who wanted to work for Abraham.

5. Those who did not accept this sign of covenant relationship were to be excluded from the life of God's people. They had refused God's offer of covenant relationship.

F. **How Did Abraham Demonstrate His Acceptance of God's Offer of Covenant Relationship?**

1. Abraham demonstrated his acceptance by believing God. He took Him at His word and lived according to God's covenant terms. This we call faith.

Laying the Foundation Summary

        2.   Abraham demonstrated his acceptance by obeying God and going into the land God had promised him.

        3.   Abraham demonstrated his acceptance even in offering back to God what was most precious to him, his own son Isaac.

G.   **How Did God's Covenant Continue After Abraham?**

        1.   The covenant and blessings of God continued through Abraham's son Isaac. Isaac was a child born to Abraham and Sarah his wife after they were too old to have children.

        2.   Isaac received the covenant sign of circumcision as required by God.

        3.   God appeared to Isaac and confirmed the covenant and the promises.

H.   **How Did God's Covenant Continue After Isaac?**

        1.   God's covenant continued through Jacob, the son of Isaac.

        2.   God chose Jacob to receive the covenant blessing even though he was not the oldest son. It is up to God to choose whom He will use to bring about His purposes.

        3.   Jacob received the covenant blessing from his father Isaac.

        4.   God changed Jacob's name to "Israel," and Israel became the father of twelve tribes who were called the "children of Israel."

II.   **Israel, Called to Be the People of God**

    A.   **Who Was the Nation of Israel?**

        1.   The children of Israel grew into the nation of Israel while they lived in the land of Egypt for over 400 years.

The Exaltation of Christ

2. The nation of Israel was God's people who were persecuted in Egypt.

3. God wanted to continue His covenant with the nation of Israel by bringing them into what He had promised to Abraham.

4. God chose Moses to lead Israel out of the bondage of Egypt and into a theocracy under God. (Theocracy—the rule of God)

B. **What Was the Relationship Between God and Israel?**

1. The relationship between God and Israel was a covenant relationship by which Israel would become a people holy to God.

2. The relationship between God and Israel was based upon the law that He gave them through Moses at Mount Sinai.

C. **What Is the Nature and Purpose of the Law God Gave to Israel?**

1. The law was a code set forth by God through Moses that represented the heart and character of a holy God.

2. The law taught Israel about sin and how to live with a holy God.

3. The law was in place to lead us to Christ.

4. The law was in man's heart from the very beginning.

D. **What Are the Ten Commandments and What Do They Teach Us? What Do They Forbid?**

1. The first commandment is: You shall have no other gods before Me (Exodus 20:3).

2. The second commandment is: You shall not make for yourself a carved image (Exodus 20:4).

3. The third commandment is: You shall not take the name of the Lord your God in vain (Exodus 20:7).

Laying the Foundation Summary

    4.   The fourth commandment is: Remember the Sabbath day, to keep it holy. (Exodus 20:8).

    5.   The fifth commandment is: Honor your father and your mother, that your days may be long upon the land which the Lord your God is giving you (Exodus 20:12).

    6.   The sixth commandment is: You shall not murder. (Exodus 20:13).

    7.   The seventh commandment is: You shall not commit adultery (Exodus 20:14).

    8.   The eighth commandment is: You shall not steal (Exodus 20:15).

    9.   The ninth commandment is: You shall not bear false witness against your neighbor (Exodus 20:16).

    10.   The tenth commandment is: You shall not covet your neighbor's house...nor anything that is your neighbor's (Exodus 20:17).

E.   **What Is the Summary of the Ten Commandments?**

    1.   The first five commandments, or table of the law, deal with our relationship with God.

    2.   The last five commandments, or second table, deal with our relationship with other people.

    3.   The summary of all the law is love—love for God and love for man.

F.   **What Are the Results of Not Keeping the Law?**

    1.   The result of not keeping the law is separation from God and a curse.

    2.   No man can be saved by keeping the law. We are saved by grace through faith alone.

    3.   No man can keep the law perfectly. But Christ took upon Himself the curse of the law so that we might inherit the blessings God promised to Abraham.

The Exaltation of Christ

Jesus was the only one ever born who walked in perfect faith and obedience.

G. **How Did God Confirm His Covenant Relationship With Israel?**

1. God spoke to Moses on Mount Sinai to establish His covenant and law with Israel.

2. Moses read all the words of the law to the people of Israel.

H. **Was Israel Able to Keep the Law and Covenant of God?**

1. Israel was never able to keep the law and the covenant with God. If man was going to be in relationship with God it would not be by the Old Covenant. God announced through the prophets that He would initiate a New Covenant.

2. The New Covenant was not written on stone tablets but in the hearts of the people.

Book 4—From Covenant to Kingdom

I. Taking Possession of the Promises of God

A. **By What Right Did the Nation of Israel Take Possession of the Land of Canaan?**

1. Israel took possession by virtue of the promises made by God to their father Abraham.

2. Israel took possession by the confirmation of God's promise through Moses.

3. Israel took possession of the land as an inheritance from God.

B. **What Did Israel Have to Do in Order to Take Possession of Their Inheritance?**

1. To take possession of their inheritance Israel had to have faith in God's word and provision.

Laying the Foundation Summary

    2.   To take possession of their inheritance Israel had to obey leaders that God placed ahead of them.

    3.   To take possession of their inheritance Israel renewed the covenant with God through the sign of circumcision.

    4.   To take possession of their inheritance Israel had to keep the law of God. There were blessings for obedience and curses for disobedience of the law.

C. **Did Israel Obey God Under Joshua and Take Possession of the Land God Promised?**

    1.   Israel obeyed God all the days of Joshua's leadership. God gave them all the land He had promised to their fathers.

    2.   Israel took possession of all the land that God promised.

    3.   Israel obeyed the law of God until after the death of Joshua.

D. **How Did God Respond to the Disobedience of the People of Israel?**

    1.   God responded to their disobedience by giving them over to the heathen nations whose gods they served.

    2.   God responded to their disobedience by showing Israel grace and mercy when they cried out to Him. He raised up judges who delivered them from the hand of their enemies.

    3.   God responded to their disobedience by sending them prophets to remind them of their relationship with God.

E. **Who Was Samuel?**

    1.   Samuel was the last "judge" of Israel and the first in the line of prophets.

The Exaltation of Christ

       2. Samuel heard the complaints of the people who wanted a king like the other nations around them had. Samuel was displeased with their request.

       3. The Lord used Samuel to set up the kingdom of Israel. It was Samuel who anointed the first two kings of Israel.

II. **Establishing the Kingdom**

   A. **Who Did the Lord Intend to Rule Over the Nation of Israel?**

       1. The Lord Himself was to be the King over Israel. It is the Lord who is King over all those who have submitted themselves to His reign.

       2. But Israel rejected the Lord who was to reign as King. They wanted a king of flesh like the nations around them had. They said that Samuel was too old and that his sons did not follow the Lord.

   B. **How Did the Lord Respond to Israel's Desire for an Earthly King?**

       1. The Lord was displeased at their request.

       2. The Lord warned the nation that earthly kings were harsh and demanding. Nevertheless, Israel, with hardened hearts, rejected God. God's warning was fulfilled.

       3. The Lord provided Saul to be king over the nation of Israel.

   C. **Who Was Saul?**

       1. Saul was the first king of Israel.

       2. Saul walked with God in the beginning of his reign and was empowered by the Spirit of God.

       3. Saul sinned against the Lord as he tried to take the role of a priest.

Laying the Foundation Summary

    4.   Saul later failed to fully obey the word of the Lord through Samuel the prophet, and the Spirit as well as the kingdom was taken from him.

    5.   Saul turned completely away from God. He sought counsel from witches and eventually died defeated, at his own hand.

D. **Who Was David? What Was His Relationship to God?**

    1.   David was the least of the sons of Jesse—a shepherd whom God chose to succeed Saul as king over Israel.

    2.   David was a "man after God's own heart." He would not be like Saul who served his own interests but would serve the Lord in faithfulness to see the kingdom reign of God established in Israel. David was a man of faith and obedience to the Lord.

    3.   David was a worshiper of God at all times. He wrote many Psalms, which were and are used to praise the Lord.

    4.   David was also a man who failed the Lord in sin but repented of his sin and was restored.

E. **What Was God's Promise to King David, and How Did It Come to Pass?**

    1.   God promised that He would establish the throne of David forever. This means that someone from his line would always sit on the throne of Israel.

    2.   Even though David's descendants and Israel failed, God fulfilled His promise through the Person of Jesus Christ, Son of David.

F. **What Was the Spiritual Significance of David's Reign?**

    1.   It was through David's reign that God prophetically revealed His spiritual purpose in Christ and in the Church. *David* is a prophetic name for Christ.

The Exaltation of Christ

      2.   David's lineage is referred to as his "house" or "tabernacle," which God promised to establish forever. It was through David's house that Jesus Christ, the Messiah, would be born.

G. **Who Was Solomon? What Was His Relationship to God?**

      1.   Solomon was King David's son who became the third king of Israel.

      2.   Solomon was charged by God to build Him a great temple. The temple was to be a place where God's glory would dwell on earth.

      3.   Solomon failed God by taking wives from heathen nations and allowing them to bring their false gods.

H. **What Was the Result of Solomon's Failing Before God?**

      1.   Solomon's kingdom was taken from him and given to one who was not in David's line. However, God preserved a "remnant" of David's kingdom through which He would fulfill His promise to David.

      2.   After 120 years of unity, Israel was divided into two kingdoms following Solomon's death.

      3.   All that Solomon built was captured or destroyed by the enemies of God.

I. **Why and How Did God Allow the Nation of Israel to Be Destroyed?**

      1.   God destroyed Israel because they did not walk in faith and obedience to Him. They chose to serve the false gods of the nations around them.

      2.   God destroyed even the remnant tribe of Judah for her unfaithfulness.

      3.   After warning the northern tribes of Israel by faithful prophets, God allowed them to be carried into captivity by Assyria.

Laying the Foundation Summary

    4. After warning the southern tribes in the nation of Judah, the Lord allowed them to be carried away into captivity in Babylon for 70 years.

  J. **How Did the Issues of Faith and Obedience Enter Into the Fate of Israel?**

    The kings that followed David in Judah were not always as faithful and obedient to the Lord as he was.

III. **The Message of the Prophets**

  A. **What Is a Prophet?**

    1. A prophet is one who speaks the word of God to His people under the inspiration of the Holy Spirit.

    2. A prophet calls the people of God to faith and obedience in the Lord.

    3. A prophet may speak of what is going to happen in the future.

    4. A prophet sometimes prophesies with musical accompaniment.

  B. **Who Were the Prophets of the Old Testament?**

    1. There was the group we call the Major Prophets.

    2. There was the group we call the Minor Prophets. (They were not called minor because of the level of importance of the messages they spoke.)

  C. **What Rules Must We Follow in Order to Understand the Words of the Prophets?**

    1. To understand the prophets we must remember that the Bible is a spiritual book. We must have the Holy Spirit's help to understand them.

    2. To understand the prophets we must read them in light of the times in which they were written. This is called historical context.

    3. To understand the prophets we must read them in terms of fulfillment in the New Testament.

The Exaltation of Christ

        4.   To understand the prophets we must read them in light of their future fulfillment.

D.   **What Was the Mission of the Prophets?**

        1.   The mission of the prophets was to call the nations of Israel and Judah back to faith and obedience to God.

        2.   The mission of the prophets was to remind the people of the covenant between the nation and their God.

E.   **What Was the Message of the Prophets?**

        1.   The message of the prophets to Israel and Judah was that they must turn from their evil ways and back to God.

        2.   The message of the prophets was that judgment would come upon those who did not repent.

        3.   The message of the prophets was that a remnant would survive the captivity.

F.   **What Did the Prophets Say Concerning Jesus Christ?**

        1.   The prophets said that out of the remnant would come the Savior of the world from the line of David.

        2.   This Savior would suffer and die to save His people from sin.

        3.   This Savior would bring them into a New Covenant that would include all people, Jews and Gentiles alike.

        4.   This Savior would establish an everlasting kingdom.

G.   **What Was the Message of the Prophets Concerning the Church?**

        1.   The prophets said that God would pour out His Spirit on those in the New Covenant.

Laying the Foundation Summary

2. The prophets said that God would rebuild the tabernacle of David through the Church. The reign of Christ from the house (tabernacle) of David would continue for all people—not just the nation of Israel.

3. The prophets said that the Church would minister in the power and anointing of the Holy Spirit to restore those saved from sin and captivity.

4. The prophets said that the Church would have dominion over evil.

5. The prophets said that the Church would be a purified and righteous people.

6. The prophets said that through the Church, the earth would be filled with the knowledge of the glory of the Lord.

7. The prophets said that Jesus Christ would return for His glorious and spotless bride, the Church.

8. The prophets said that worship would be restored in the Church.

IV. **Restoring the Remnant of Israel**

    A. **For What Purpose Did God Preserve a Remnant of Israel?**

        1. God always preserves a "remnant," a holy seed through which to continue His purposes and carry out His word.

        2. God preserved the remnant to prepare the way for Jesus Christ to be born.

        3. God preserved a remnant to restore Jerusalem.

        4. God preserved a remnant to restore His house.

        5. God preserved the remnant to restore His law.

The Exaltation of Christ

B. How Did God Preserve the Remnant of Israel?

1. God called the remnant to return from their captivity back to Israel in fulfillment of His word through the prophets.

2. God chose Cyrus, the king of Persia, to destroy Babylon and to allow the Jews to return to Israel following 70 years (606 B.C. to 536 B.C.) of captivity.

C. Who Did God Choose to Lead This Remnant? What Were Their Roles?

1. Zerubbabel was the governor when the temple was rebuilt in 536-516 B.C. He was also a direct descendant of King David through whom Jesus Christ would be born. He represents Jesus Christ who would build His Church.

2. Joshua was the high priest during the time of Zerubbabel.

3. Haggai was responsible for re-starting the building of the temple after it was stopped out of fear for 15 years. He prophetically saw the glory of the Church, God's ultimate temple.

4. Zechariah was another prophet who encouraged the rebuilding of the temple. He had a revelation of righteousness being restored through Christ.

5. Ezra was a priestly scribe who returned to Jerusalem with Zerubbabel. He was a key figure during the time of Nehemiah in restoring the law to the returning remnant of Israel.

6. Nehemiah was a trusted servant (cupbearer) to the king of Persia. He was allowed by the king to return to Jerusalem to complete the rebuilding of that city by repairing the gates and walls.

D. What Was the Opposition That the Returning Remnant Faced As They Rebuilt Jerusalem?

1. The remnant faced satanic opposition.

2. The remnant faced opposition within the walls of Jerusalem.

Laying the Foundation Summary

        3. The remnant faced opposition outside the walls of Jerusalem.

E. **What Lessons Can Be Learned From the Return of the Remnant?**

        1. We learn that we must continue to do the will and work of God despite opposition.

        2. We learn that we can only work effectively when our hearts are devoted to the work and the leaders that God has placed ahead of us.

        3. We learn that it is God who is worthy of our praise when we do His work.

        4. We learn that God sends His word ahead of his work through the prophets.

F. **What Meaning Does the Restoration of the Remnant Hold for Us Today?**

        1. The restoration of the temple points to Jesus Christ building His Church out of living stones.

        2. The restoration of the wall points to the security that we now have in Christ Jesus through repentance, baptism, and the infilling of the Holy Spirit.

        3. The restoration of the law points to the eternal nature of the law that is now written on the hearts of those in the New Covenant through Jesus Christ.

Book 5—The New Covenant

I. **The New Covenant**

    A. **What Is the New Covenant?**

        1. The New Covenant is the agreement that God offers to all men to restore right relationship through the Person of Jesus Christ, His Son.

The Exaltation of Christ

  2. The New Covenant was written about by the prophets who lived under the Old Covenant.

  3. The New Covenant abolished the Old Covenant because Israel was not able to keep it.

  4. The New Covenant fulfills the purpose of God, which is to take away sin and restore righteous relationship.

B. **Who Is the Mediator of This New Covenant?**

  1. Jesus Christ is the Mediator, the One who brings man back into fellowship with God.

  2. It is the blood of Jesus that guarantees the New Covenant.

C. **Where Do We Read About the New Covenant?**

We read about the New Covenant in the second part of the Bible called the New Testament.

D. **How Do We Enter Into the New Covenant?**

  1. We enter into the New Covenant through repentance—turning away from our old self-centered and sinful ways—and turning in faith to Jesus Christ.

  2. We enter the covenant by receiving the sign of the New Covenant, which is baptism.

II. **The Person of Jesus Christ**

 A. **Who Is Jesus Christ?**

  1. Jesus Christ is both the Son of God and the Son of man.

  2. Jesus Christ is the only way of salvation for man.

  3. Jesus Christ is the Messiah of Israel. The name *Jesus* means "Yahweh is salvation." His name *Christ* means the "anointed one."

Laying the Foundation Summary

- **B. Why Must We Understand the Person of Jesus?**
    1. We must understand the Person of Jesus because He is the very source of Christianity.
    2. We must understand the Person of Jesus because without Him there is no Christianity. We cannot separate Jesus from His teaching.

III. The Nature of Jesus Christ

- **A. What Two Natures Are United Only in Jesus Christ?**
    1. Jesus Christ was fully human. He was God incarnate (in the flesh).
    2. Jesus Christ was fully God. He was called the Son of God.
    3. Only in Jesus do these two natures, divinity and humanity, unite.

- **B. How Do We Know That Jesus Christ Was Man?**
    1. We know that Jesus was man because He was born of a woman.
    2. We know that Jesus was man because He grew and developed like any other human.
    3. We know that Jesus was man because He had human flesh and appearance.
    4. We know that Jesus was man because He had human needs and emotions.
    5. We know that Jesus was man because He had a human name.

- **C. How Do We Know That Jesus Christ Is God?**
    1. We know that Jesus is God because He was given divine titles.
    2. We know that Jesus is God because of the unique qualities that belonged to Him.

3. We know that Jesus is God because He does the works of God.

4. We know that Jesus is God because He was worshiped as God.

5. We know that Jesus is God because He displayed sovereignty and authority.

D. Why Is It Important That Jesus Was Fully God?

1. Jesus had to be fully God because only God could carry the burden of God's wrath.

2. Jesus had to be fully God because only God could save man.

3. Jesus had to be fully God to be Mediator between God and man to bring us back to God.

E. Why Is It Important That Jesus Is Fully Human?

1. Jesus had to be fully human in order to demonstrate the perfect faith and obedience that had been lost at the fall of Adam. Jesus was referred to as the second Adam.

2. Jesus had to be fully human to be a sympathetic High Priest for us.

3. Jesus had to be fully human in order to die as a substitute sacrifice for man.

F. For What Three Offices Was Jesus Christ Anointed?

1. Jesus was anointed as Prophet to reveal to us the nature of God through the word of God.

2. Jesus was anointed as Priest as He went to the cross to present Himself as a sacrifice to satisfy the justice of God. He restores our relationship with God and then becomes our intercessor at the throne.

3. Jesus was anointed as King to rule over His people and to destroy the power of the enemy.

Laying the Foundation Summary

IV. **The Humiliation of Jesus Christ**

    A. **How Did Jesus Christ Humble Himself?**

        1. Jesus humbled Himself by emptying Himself of His power and position in Heaven.

        2. Jesus humbled Himself by being born of a woman in a stable.

        3. Jesus humbled Himself by being under the law as all other men.

        4. Jesus humbled Himself by living with poverty and suffering.

        5. Jesus humbled Himself by being persecuted by men and forsaken by God.

        6. Jesus humbled Himself by suffering crucifixion, taking upon Himself the sins of man and the wrath of God.

        7. Jesus humbled Himself by death and burial for three days.

    B. **What Are the Results of Christ's Humiliation?**

        1. Through the humiliation of Christ we are redeemed, purchased back from the power of sin and satan. Satan had the power of accusation, sickness, fear, and death.

        2. Through the humiliation of Christ we are redeemed from all sin.

        3. Through the humiliation of Christ we are redeemed from death.

        4. Through the humiliation of Christ we are redeemed from the curse of the law (the results of our disobedience to the law).

    C. **How Has Christ Redeemed Us?**

        1. Christ has redeemed us through His own innocent blood.

The Exaltation of Christ

    2.   Christ has redeemed us by making atonement for our sin, (at-one-ment), bringing us back into relationship with God.

    3.   Christ has redeemed us by taking our place and paying our penalty.

    4.   Christ has redeemed all who accept Him and has condemned all who refuse Him.

Book 6—Jesus Christ, Servant of God

I. **Wounded for Our Transgressions**

  A. **What Are Transgressions?**

    1.   Transgressions are willful and defiling acts of sin. They are stains of rebellion.

    2.   Transgressions are a "going beyond" the bounds of God's laws and ways.

  B. **What Is Meant by "Wounded for Our Transgressions"?**

    1.   The law of God demands the shedding of blood to forgive man's sin. This word *wounded* could also be translated "pierced," which points to Christ's death by crucifixion.

    2.   Jesus became the sacrifice and shed His own blood for the forgiveness of our sins.

    3.   Jesus took our place and became sin for us.

  C. **How Does God Forgive Our Sins?**

    1.   God forgives and forgets our sins when we confess them.

    2.   God forgives our sins when we turn from them. (The Bible calls this repentance.)

    3.   God forgives our sins when we ask Him for forgiveness.

Laying the Foundation Summary

- **D. How Can We Be Sure That Our Sins Are Forgiven?**

    1. WORD: We can be sure our sins are forgiven because the Word of God says they are forgiven when we believe on the name of Jesus Christ.

    2. WITNESS: We can be sure our sins are forgiven because of the witness of the Holy Spirit. God sends the Holy Spirit to assure us that we now belong to Him. Now we are led by the Spirit rather than our own desires.

    3. WATER: We can be sure that our sins are forgiven as we demonstrate new faith and obedience by going through water baptism. (This is a circumcision of heart.)

II. Bruised for Our Iniquities

- **A. What Is Iniquity and How Does It Differ From Sin?**

    1. Transgressions are acts of sin while iniquity is the evil nature born in us.

    2. Iniquity is the sinful self-serving attitude that breeds transgressions.

    3. Transgressions refer to the outward acts of sin. Iniquity refers to the inward and crooked bent toward sin.

- **B. Where and When Did We Acquire Iniquity?**

    1. We acquired iniquity from our forefathers.

    2. Iniquity is referred to as "the old man" or "the body of sin."

- **C. What Does the Bible Mean by "Bruised for Our Iniquities"?**

    1. To be bruised is to be utterly crushed as under the weight of our iniquity.

    2. Jesus Christ was crushed for our iniquity that we might be freed from the power of the sinful nature we inherited from our forefathers.

The Exaltation of Christ

- **D. Why Must We Be Purified From Iniquity?**
    1. We must be freed from iniquity because God looks at our hearts.
    2. We must be purified from iniquity because our hearts are the source of sin.
    3. We must be purified from iniquity to live a life that pleases God.

- **E. How Can We Be Freed From the Curse of Iniquity?**
    1. We can be freed from iniquity by confessing our unrighteousness to God.
    2. We can be freed from iniquity by turning from sinful ways.
    3. We can be freed from iniquity by being baptized in water, separating us from our sinful nature, and entering into our new nature in Christ Jesus.

- **F. How Can We Be Sure That Our Iniquity Will Be Taken Away From Our Children and Ourselves?**

    We can be sure because God's Word tells us that Jesus has redeemed us from all iniquity.

III. Chastised for Our Peace

- **A. What Does It Mean That Jesus Was Chastised for Our Peace?**
    1. *Chastised* means "corrected or disciplined." Men's hardened hearts could not receive the instruction of God; therefore Jesus suffered discipline for us.
    2. *Chastisement* means "direction with a rod of correction." Jesus took the blows of our instruction.

- **B. What Is Peace?**
    1. Peace is a state of wholeness, completeness, and rest.
    2. Peace is the total absence of fear.

Laying the Foundation Summary

        3. Peace is a state of rest and harmony between people and God.

  C. **What Is Peace With God?**

        1. Peace with God is a restored relationship with God through Jesus Christ.

        2. Peace with God is a total dependence upon God resulting in the rest of God.

        3. Peace is a characteristic of the Kingdom of God.

        4. Peace is a fruit of the Holy Spirit.

  D. **How Will Peace With God Affect Our Lives?**

        1. Peace with God provides us with an inner quietness.

        2. Peace with God provides freedom from the feelings of guilt and shame.

        3. Peace with God gives us strength in the midst of trouble.

        4. Peace with God leads to peace with others in the Body of Christ.

IV. **Scourged for Our Healing**

  A. **What Does "With His Stripes We Are Healed" Mean?**

        1. This means that the sickness and disease of a fallen world were beaten into the body of Jesus.

        2. It means that we are joined with Christ in His victory over sin, sickness, and death.

  B. **How Did Sickness and Disease Enter the World?**

        1. Sickness entered the world when Adam sinned against God.

        2. Sickness entered the world when man gave dominion over to satan. Satan uses sickness and disease to destroy man, whom God loves.

The Exaltation of Christ

C. What Is the Curse of the Law?

1. The curse of the Law was the consequences of disobedience to God's Law.

2. The curse of the Law consists of every plague and sickness that results from disobedience to God.

D. How Does the Death of Jesus Christ Heal Us?

1. Jesus took upon Himself all the curses of sin, which include sickness and disease.

2. Jesus destroyed the power of satan over man.

E. Why Is There Still Sickness in the World Today?

1. There is still sickness in the world because people do not realize that Jesus Christ purchased healing for all men.

2. There is still sickness in the world because satan has taken advantage of our ignorance concerning our healing in Christ.

F. How Is It Possible to Be Healed?

1. We can be healed by believing and trusting in God's word, that He will do as He promised.

2. We can be healed by confessing, speaking the truth.

G. How May We Receive Healing?

1. We may receive healing by personal confession and prayer.

2. We may receive healing by the laying on of hands.

3. We may receive healing by the prayer of the elders.

4. We may receive healing in the presence of the Lord in worship and praise.

H. What May Prevent Our Healing?

1. Healing may be prevented by unbelief.

2. Healing may be prevented by unconfessed sins.

Laying the Foundation Summary

          3. Healing may be prevented by bitterness we hold against another.

I. **Why May Healing Be Delayed?**

          1. Healing may be delayed to teach us patience and understanding of God.

          2. Healing may be delayed in order to fulfill God's purpose.

Book 7—The Exaltation of Christ

I. The Exaltation of Christ

    A. **What Do the Scriptures Teach Us About Christ's Descent Into Hell?**

          1. Jesus, after His crucifixion, went to preach to spirits of people who died and were in Hades. They had an opportunity to accept Christ and be in the presence of God.

          2. Jesus preached to those in Hades so that the gospel would be preached to all regions, and so that He might fill all things.

    B. **What Is the Significance of the Resurrection of Christ?**

          1. The Scriptures teach us that three days after Jesus died He was raised from the dead.

          2. The Scriptures tell us that Christ was raised with a glorified physical body as the firstfruits from the dead. He had a body free of the corruption that resulted from the Fall of Adam.

    C. **What Assurances Do We Have As a Result of Christ's Resurrection?**

          1. The resurrection assures us that Jesus Christ is the Son of God.

The Exaltation of Christ

2. The resurrection assures us that all of the words Jesus spoke were true.

3. The resurrection assures us that the Father approved His work of redemption and accepted His sacrifice.

4. The resurrection assures us that believers in Christ have the hope of eternal life.

5. It assures us that believers will receive perfect and incorruptible bodies like Jesus.

D. What Is the Significance of Christ's Ascension?

1. The ascension of Christ is significant in that He leads the way for us into the glory of God.

2. The ascension of Christ is significant in that He received honor and glory, being seated at the right hand of God. This is the place of all authority and power.

3. The ascension of Christ to the right hand of God means that all other powers have been put under His feet.

4. The ascension of Christ gives us hope of living eternally in a place prepared for us by the Lord Himself.

5. The ascension of Christ assures us that we will rule and reign with Him.

6. The ascension of Christ provides a new focus on the throne of God rather than the circumstances of our earthly life.

E. How and When Will Christ Return to the Earth?

1. Christ will return to the earth in the same glory with which He ascended.

2. Christ will return in righteous judgment of the living and the dead.

Laying the Foundation Summary

        3.   Christ will return at a time known only by God. We are to watch for His return.

   F.   **What Are We to Do Until Christ's Return?**

        We are to do the business of the Kingdom until Christ's return.

II.   **Jesus Christ and the Kingdom of God**

   A.   **What Is the Kingdom of God?**

        1.   The Kingdom of God is the present reality of God's rule over all who submit to His Lordship.

        2.   The Kingdom of God is the realm of His sovereign authority and dominion. This realm will continue to increase until all is subjected to Jesus Christ as King.

        3.   The Kingdom of God is ruled by Jesus Christ the King.

   B.   **How Was the Kingdom Announced?**

        1.   The Kingdom of God was announced in the Old Testament.

        2.   The Kingdom of God was announced in the New Testament.

   C.   **How Did Jesus Introduce the Kingdom of God?**

        1.   Jesus preached the Kingdom of God from the very beginning of His ministry.

        2.   Jesus preached that the Kingdom of God had come as a present reality, not just a hope for the future. The prophecies concerning the Kingdom were now fulfilled in Christ.

   D.   **How Was the Kingdom of God Manifested in the New Testament?**

        1.   The Kingdom of God was manifested in the ministry of Jesus Christ.

The Exaltation of Christ

      2.   The Kingdom of God was manifested by authority over sickness and demons.

      3.   The Kingdom of God was manifested in the outpouring of the Holy Spirit. The Church became witness of the reality of Christ's enthronement and present rule.

E. **How Was the Kingdom of God Described?**

      1.   The Kingdom of God is described in the Sermon on the Mount and the Beatitudes found in Matthew 5. (What we are "to be" in the Kingdom)

      2.   The Kingdom of God is described in the parables Jesus taught.

F. **How Do We Enter the Kingdom of God?**

      1.   We enter the Kingdom of God by trusting Jesus Christ as Lord and Savior. Those called into the Kingdom are the *ekklesia*, the Church. The Church is the community of those who respond to God's calling into the Kingdom.

      2.   We enter the Kingdom by obedience to the King, Jesus Christ.

More Titles by Dr. Mark Hanby

YOU HAVE NOT MANY FATHERS
"My son, give me your heart." So says the proverb, echoing the heart and passion of our Father in heaven. God has spiritual "dads" all over the world whom He has filled with wisdom, knowledge, compassion, and most of all, love for those young in the faith. You do not have to go through your life untrained and unloved; uncared for and forgotten. There are fathers in Christ who are waiting to pour all they have into your heart, as Elijah did for Elisha. "My son, give me your heart."
ISBN 1-56043-166-0

YOU HAVE NOT MANY FATHERS STUDY GUIDE
ISBN 0-7684-2036-9

THE HOUSE THAT GOD BUILT
Beyond whatever man can desire is a God-given pattern for the life of the Church. Here Dr. Hanby unfolds practical applications from the design of the Tabernacle that allow us to become the house God is building today.
ISBN 1-56043-091-5

THE HOUSE THAT GOD BUILT STUDY GUIDE
ISBN 0-7684-2048-2

THE RENEWING OF THE HOLY GHOST
Do you need renewal? Everything in the natural, from birds to blood cells, must either undergo a process of renewal or enter into death. Our spiritual life is no different. With this book, your renewal can begin today!
ISBN 1-56043-031-1

ANOINTING THE UNSANCTIFIED
The anointing is more than a talented performance or an emotional response. In this book, Dr. Hanby details the essential ingredients of directional relationship that allow the Spirit of God to flow down upon the Body of Christ—and from us to the needs of a dying world.
ISBN 1-56043-071-0

PERCEIVING THE WHEEL OF GOD
On the potter's wheel, a lump of clay yields to a necessary process of careful pressure and constant twisting. Similarly, the form of true faith is shaped by a trusting response to God in a suffering situation. This book offers essential understanding for victory through the struggles of life.
ISBN 1-56043-109-1

Available at your local Christian bookstore.

For more information and sample chapters, visit www.destinyimage.com